SEV
LAST W

SEVEN
LAST WORDS

Timothy Radcliffe O.P.

burns & oates

Burns & Oates
A Continuum Imprint
The Tower Building
11 York Road
London SE1 7NX

15 East 26th Street
New York
NY 10010

www.continuumbooks.com

© Timothy Radcliffe O.P. 2004

'Musée des Beaux Arts', and 'The More Loving One', from *Collected Shorter Poems 1927–1957* by W. H. Auden, are reproduced by kind permission of Faber and Faber Limited.

First published 2004

British Library Cataloguing-in-Publication Data
A catalogue record for this book is available from the British Library.
ISBN 0 8601 2365 0
Designed and typeset by Benn Linfield
Printed and bound by Cromwell Press, Trowbridge, Wiltshire

Contents

Foreword

In the beginning was the Word

On the evening of 7 December 1993, I had just arrived in Jerusalem from Rome to visit the *Ecole Biblique*, the Dominican centre for Biblical studies. I had not even unpacked when I received a phone call to say that my father was dying. Immediately I flew to England and I was able to have a few last days with him before he died in hospital, surrounded by his family. He had a passionate love of music and so we bought him a Walkman for use in the ward. I asked him what CDs he would like to have and he told me to bring Mozart's *Requiem* and Haydn's *Seven Last Words*. This was his way of preparing himself for death. I had flown from the place where, according to the Gospels, Jesus spoke these last words to be with my father as he lived his own passion with their help.

We can trace back the devotion to the Seven Last Words of Jesus on the Cross to the twelfth century. Various authors had woven one harmonious account of Jesus' life out of the four Gospels. This brought together his last words on the cross, seven phrases, which became a topic of meditation. These last words were commented on by St Bonaventure and popularized by the Franciscans. They were immensely important in late medieval piety, and were linked with meditation on the seven wounds of Christ, and seen as remedies for the Seven Deadly Sins.[1] According to the Hours of St Bede, whoever meditated on these words of Jesus would be saved and Our Lady would appear to him thirty days before his death.

However, when I was asked to preach on the Seven Last Words of Jesus, at Seattle Cathedral on Good Friday 2002, I must admit that I hesitated. They appeared to belong to a gloomy spirituality, which dwelt on suffering and sin, and with which I could not easily identify. Of course the gospel says that we are to take up our cross daily and follow Christ, but too often this has spilt over into a Christianity that seemed to me to be joyless, life-denying and with even a hint of masochism. St John of the Cross says that 'the soul which really longs for divine wisdom, first longs for suffering, that it may enter more deeply into the thicket of the cross.'[2] I confess that I have no longing to suffer at all! I was reminded of these gloomy words from *Richard II*:

Let's talk of graves, of worms, and epitaphs;
Make dust our paper, and with rainy eyes
Write sorrow on the bosom of the earth.
Let's choose executors, and talk of wills.[3]

My faith is about life, the birth of a child and victory over death. Of course this necessarily passes through Good Friday, but why remain focused on that moment? I had too often encountered suffering and death, especially during my travels around the Order in places like Rwanda and Burundi, to be ignorant of its awful violence. I had been with many brethren as they died and seen the limits of what can be said but only shown. And I had doubts about whether one should preach even *one* sermon on Good Friday, let alone seven. Faced with the horror of the death of the Son of God, its scandalous nonsense, then what is there to say? It marks the end of words. Must one always be talking? All one can do is to wait for Easter. However, I accepted to preach on the Seven Last Words in memory of my beloved father who shared his faith with me. These words had given him strength in the face of death. What might they give me?

Last words are especially fascinating. Human beings are speaking animals. For us to be alive is to be in communication. Death is not just the cessation of bodily life. It is silence. So what we say in the face of imminent silence is revealing. It may be resigned; Ned Kelly, the Australian bank robber, managed, 'Such is life' just before he was executed. Lord Palmerston, 'The last thing that I shall do is to die,' is more defiant or just pragmatic. One may be gloriously mistaken, like the civil war general who said of the enemy sharpshooters, 'They could not hit an elephant at this distance.' Few of us manage the grandeur of the Emperor Vespasian's 'Woe is me; I think that I am becoming a god.' Pitt the younger is supposed to have said, 'Oh my country, how I leave my country,' but the more reliable tradition gives us, 'I think that I could eat one of Bellamy's meat pies.' In fact many dying people ask for food and drink. St Thomas Aquinas asked for fresh herrings, which were miraculously provided, and Anton Chekhov announced that it was never too late for a glass of champagne.

In this little book we are concerned not just with the last words of a man, the last things that Jesus, a first-century Jew, happened to say. We see the Word of God spoken in the face of silence. As Christians we believe that everything exists and is sustained by that Word which was from the beginning. It is the meaning of all our lives. As John wrote in the Prologue to his Gospel, 'In him was life and the life was the light of humanity' (1.4). What is at issue for us is not just the meaning of his life but of every life. When he was silenced, then were all human words entombed with him?

Our faith in the Resurrection is not just that this man who died was brought back to life. The Word was not silenced. These seven last words live. The tomb did not engulf them. This is not just because they were heard, remembered and written down, like the last words of Socrates. It means that the silence of the tomb was broken for ever, and those words were not the last. 'The light shines in the darkness and the darkness has not overcome it' (John 1.5).

When martyrs face death, they claim the right to speak. They may protest their innocence or preach their faith, but always in the face of silence they wish their words to be heard, because the Word itself was not silenced and never will be. The early martyrs often died because they refused to hand over the gospel words. They would not be, in the literal sense of the word, traitors of these words of life. These are the words that are entrusted to us. The Roman Governor asks Euplius why he will not surrender these books. 'Because I am a Christian and it is forbidden to give them up. Better it is to die than surrender them. In them is eternal life. Whoever gives them up loses eternal life.'[4]

For Christians what is at issue is not just whether these words of Jesus are true, but ultimately whether any human words have meaning at all, even of those who do not share our faith. Are our attempts to make sense of our existence vain, in the face of that ultimate silence when all the Universe will grow cold and dead? Do we live between the Creation and the Kingdom, or between just the Big Bang and the final silence?

The Christian story is a drama about words and their meaning, God's Word and ours. It begins with the Word through which everything came to be. In the Middle Ages, theologians loved to dwell on one dramatic moment in the story. When the angel Gabriel appeared to Mary and made the announcement of Jesus' conception, then would Mary say Yes? They loved to imagine Mary hesitating while the whole of humanity nervously waits to see what she will say. Adam and Eve, and all dead urge her on. The whole of creation holds its breath. The coming of the Word depends upon her word. St Bernard begs her, 'Answer O Virgin, answer the angel speedily ... Speak the word and receive the Word; offer what is yours and conceive what is of God ... Why Delay? Why tremble? Believe, speak, receive.'[5] This epitomizes our immense human responsibility as those who speak words. Our words give life or death; they create or destroy. The climax of this drama is Jesus' last words on the cross. We treasure them because here is rooted our faith that human words do indeed reach after and touch some ultimate destiny and purpose. Our words may be inadequate and barely touch the mystery, but they are not empty.

In Robert Bolt's play, *A Man for All Seasons*, when Meg tried to persuade her father, St Thomas More, to take the oath because he could disavow the words in his mind, he replied, 'What is an oath but words we say to God? When a man takes an oath, Meg, he's holding his own self in his own hands. Like water. And if he opens his fingers *then* – he needn't hope to find himself again.'[6] Our faith is not just that human existence has a particular meaning, but that it has meaning at all, which transcends all our words. In this trust we may find allies and teachers in those who hold other faiths or none. These seven last words invite us to believe that words do matter. And the most fundamental conflict is not with those who find their faith in other words but with those who hold that nothing has any meaning at all. So whoever cares for words and cherishes meaning can help us hear the Word, which is the life and light of all human beings. Czeslaw Milosz wrote, 'Poetry by its essence has always been on the side of life.'[7] And Seamus Heaney talks of poetry's 'function as an agent of possible transformation, of evolution towards that more radiant and generous life which the imagination desires.'[8]

When I visited the room in the University in which the Jesuit martyrs of El Salvador had been murdered, I saw that their assassins had also shot their books. Kittel's *Theological Dictionary of the New Testament* was riddled with bullet holes. It was open at the article on the Holy Spirit, the one whose inspiration is in all the words of the gospel. The hatred of these murderers was not just for these priests but for their words, and yet these men filled with hatred must also have been impelled by some blind hunger for meaning too.

In May 2003 I was taken to the Tuol Sleng genocide centre in Phnom Penh, Cambodia. It was one of hundreds of such places in which the Pol Pot regime eliminated its victims. The signs around the centre all insisted that there must be complete silence. Any sound was instantly punishable by death. This silence was the first shadow of the killing fields. The walls of the cells are lined with thousands of photographs of the silenced. Some of them look at the camera with blank faces, and some, especially the young, smile as if hoping for a response. Only one of them came out alive.

Usually the attack on words takes a less dramatic form. Evil can make language banal. It subverts its beauty and nuance. It trivializes our words. Herbert McCabe wrote,

> It is entirely appropriate that Hitler's table talk should have been so boring. Bad, cheap behaviour devalues the structures of human meaning in the way that bad cheap prose devalues the languages. There is an appearance of communication concealing a failure to express oneself, to give and realize oneself. If I am right in saying that life is constituted by communication then such behaviour diminishes life or diminishes my existence.[9]

This is a time of incredible creativity for English literature. The English language is being stretched by bright young novelists and poets from all sorts of ethnic groups within Britain, and from all over the world. The language is alive and young still. And yet often in the media one sees it degraded and trivialized, used carelessly and without attention to distinction and nuance. All this subverts human communion. When I returned to live in England after nine years abroad, I was surprised to hear almost everyone speaking Estuary English. The spread of this new *lingua franca* must surely be motivated by a good desire to overthrow the divisions which used to fracture English society. I grew up in a society in which one could tell someone's class the moment they began to speak. Language was not only a way of being in communion but of asserting separation and of claiming superiority. Thanks be to God, this is ever less the case. But if our desire for a classless society takes the form of the degradation of our common language, then we are undermining the means whereby we may make communion. The trivialization of the language thwarts our ability to make a common life with those who are different. If we see communion only as the solidarity of those who are the same, then of course subtlety is not needed. As one can hear in the House of Commons, it is enough to grunt and bray, to cheer and boo.

George Steiner wrote a beautiful book called *Real Presences*. The subtitle was *Is there anything in what we say?* It explored the breaking of the covenant between words and world during the last hundred years or more, the loss of our confidence that our words mean anything at all. In these seven last sayings of Jesus we witness the ultimate contest between words and silence, meaning and nonsense, and believe that the victory has been won.

In 1985 Brian Keenan went to the Lebanon to teach English. He was kidnapped and held prisoner for four and a half years. For the first months he was in solitary confinement and often in the dark. Then he was often sustained by words. He scribbled words on every scrap of paper that he could find, or on the walls, to save himself from insanity, to prove that he existed. He often wrote poems, since these would be hard for his captors to decipher. He was sustained by words that had lain hidden in his memory but which at this moment swam into consciousness and gave him life. During one session of confrontation with his captors,

> Blake's aphorism swam into my head: 'The tigers of wrath are wiser than the horses of instruction' and with that thought I silently hummed to myself 'Bring me my bow of burning gold, bring me my arrows of desire', and at the same time pulsating in the back of my head came the words 'Yea, though I walk in the valley of the shadow of death, I will fear no evil.' [10]

These words kept him sane and alive. These last words of Jesus may lodge in our minds and hearts and sustain us whatever we may face: failure, loss, silence and death.

Various incidents of the passion narratives, such as the dividing of Jesus' clothes and his final thirst, are said to happen 'to fulfil the scriptures'. This may sound odd to our ears, as if Jesus were an actor who was following a series of stage instructions: 'Now is the moment when I must say that I am thirsty'. Clearly this is not so, and yet these references are reminders that a drama is indeed being enacted on Calvary. The Romans crucified thousands of people. A body hanging from a tree must have been a common sight, especially in times of political unrest. And so Jesus' death may have looked just like any old execution, without special significance, one of those things that just happens. For us Jesus' cross is the centre of innumerable paintings, mosaics, sculptures and carvings, which are placed at the heart of our most holy places. But the evangelists knew that it might not have seemed like that at the time, but rather something unremarkable, happening in a corner, on the edge of a rather unimportant city in a minor province of the Empire. In his poem 'Musée des Beaux Arts' Auden tells us that:

About suffering they were never wrong,
The Old Masters: how well they understood
Its human position; how it takes place
While someone else is eating or opening a window or just walking
        dully along;
How, when the aged are reverently, passionately waiting
For the miraculous birth, there always must be
Children who did not specially want it to happen, skating
On a pond at the edge of the wood:

They never forgot
That even the dreadful martyrdom must run its course
Anyhow in a corner, some untidy spot
Where dogs go on with their doggy life and the torturer's horse
Scratches its innocent behind on a tree.[11]

These references to the fulfilment of the scriptures show us that though for the passerby at the time nothing especially important may appeared to have been happening – just another troublemaker getting his comeuppance – yet it was indeed the long awaited climax in the drama of God's relationship with humanity. What was at issue was all the sacred writings, and indeed all the words we ever use to fumble for meaning.

Seven last words: in the Bible seven is the number of perfection. God created the world and rested on the seventh day, the day of completion and fulfilment. These seven words belong to God's completion of that creation. I was astonished to discover that they have their own beautiful structure. They begin with words addressed to the Father, find their centre in a cry at the absence of that Father, and return to address Him again at the end. The words that Jesus addresses to us are held within that relationship with his Father, just as it is there that we shall find our home, within the life of the Trinity. We nestle within that divine conversation. And the words that Jesus addresses to those at the foot of the cross grow in intimacy, as if death draws him nearer to us rather than taking him away. Jesus addresses us first as a King, and then as our brother, before entering most intimately into our desolation and loss.

Seven words, but it is all the speaking of one Word of life that comes to completion in the Resurrection. In the words of William Saint-Thierry, addressed to the Father: 'Everything he did and everything he said on earth, even the insults, the spitting, the buffeting, the cross and the grave, all that was nothing but yourself speaking in the Son, appealing to us by your love, and stirring up our love for you.'[12]

Because these seven words are the speaking of one Word of life, then they can only be understood in the light of the Resurrection. When the Word rose from the tomb it was not just the ratification of the words on the cross. It was more than a sign that he had been right all along. It is then that these words find the fullness of their meaning. For example, the first word is 'Father, forgive them for they know not what they do.' The Resurrection does more than confirm these words, that we can trust that the Father will indeed forgive us. We are shown what forgiveness is, that it is more than forgetting. It is Easter transformation, God's irrepressible fertility, an empty tomb.

Each meditation on these seven words is accompanied by an image of the cross, with a few words of explanation. I discovered that I do happen to have seven crosses in my room, and by happy chance, and without too much forcing, they each illuminate one of Jesus' last words. Each of these, except the last, is a gift. Three of these crosses are gifts from Latin America. This is not because Latin Americans are more generous than other people. It reflects the deep centrality of Good Friday in the spirituality of that continent. Centuries of colonialism and of poverty make Easter seem a long time coming.

It may seem strange to give someone a cross as a sign of friendship. But I discovered that pondering on the cross did not make me gloomy. To live under its shadow is not life-denying or joyless. Each of these crosses is for me an invitation to hear the Word that broke death's silence and lived. My father was right. This is not to say that death is unimportant or without pain, a mere passing through a veil. Herbert McCabe, OP, wrote:

> Death, human death is an outrage ... Most people will agree that there is something shocking in the death of a child, who has not had a chance even to life out her whole human life-cycle; but I think that, in one way, every death cuts off a story that has infinite possibilities ahead of it.[13]

Each of these crosses confronts us with the outrage that is Christ's death, and helps us to see already there the beginning of a new word of life.

1 Cf. Eamon Duffy, *The Stripping of the Altars*, New Haven, 1992, pp. 248ff.

2 *A reading from the Spiritual Canticle*, Red. B, str. 37.

3 Act 3, sc. 2, l.145.

4 *The Acts of the Christian Martyrs* intro and trans. Herbert Musurillo, Oxford, 1972, p. 317.

5 'In Praise of the Virgin Mary', Hom. 4.8.

6 New York, 1960, p. 140.

7 'The Real and the Paradigms', *Poetry Australia*, No. 72, October 1979, p. 24, quoted in Seamus Heaney, *The Redress of Poetry*, London, 1995, p. 158.

8 Heaney, *The Redress of Poetry*, p. 114.

9 *Law, Love and Language*, London, 1968, p. 100, reprinted 2003.

10 *An Evil Cradling*, London, 1992, p. 238.

11 *Collected Shorter Poems 1927–1957*, London, 1966, p. 123.

12 The treatise *On Contemplating God*, Nn. 10.

13 *Hope*, London, 1987, p. 24f.

A cross by Michael Finn

The Words

1. 'Forgive them, for they know not what they do.'
Luke 23.34

The first word given to us today is of forgiveness. Forgiveness comes before the crucifixion, before the insults and the death. Forgiveness is always first. Maybe we could not cope with listening to the passion of Christ if we did not begin with forgiveness. Before we ever sin, we are forgiven. We do not have to earn it. We do not even have to be sorry. Forgiveness is there, waiting for us.

This sounds very beautiful, but might it not also be a little patronizing? It may seem to make our acts unimportant. Some friends of mine invited me to go and have a rest with them a few weeks ago. They have charming young twins, and a theory that these twins must be allowed to do whatever they want. They could smash things, shout and scream, and change their minds every two minutes. I returned home having enjoyed myself enormously but giving thanks for celibacy. The theory was that they would grow up with a deep feeling of security, knowing that they would be loved whatever they did. I wondered. Might they not also come to think that their actions were unimportant? If you know that you are going to be forgiven whatever you do, then why bother to try to be good? 'Dear old Timothy; he has just murdered another of the brethren. It is so tedious, but the dear Lord will forgive him so it does not matter.'

Forgiveness comes first. That is the scandal of the gospel. But it does not mean that God does not take seriously what we do. God does not forget that we crucified his Son. We do not put it out of our minds. Indeed on Good Friday we gather to listen to the passion and death of Christ, and to remember that humanity rejected, humiliated and murdered the Son of God. It is because of forgiveness that we can dare to remember that most terrible deed.

Forgiveness is not God forgetting Good Friday. It is the Father raising the Son on Easter Sunday. If forgiveness were forgetting then God would have to suffer the most acute amnesia, but it is God's unimaginable creativity, which takes what we have done and makes it fruitful. The medieval image of God's forgiveness was the flowering of the cross. The cross is the ugly sign of torture. It is the symbol of humanity's ability to reject love and to do what is utterly sterile. But the artists of the Middle Ages showed this cross flowering on Easter

Sunday, as in the apse of San Clemente in Rome, which illustrates the third of Jesus' last words. The dead wood put out tendrils and flowers. Forgiveness makes the dead live and the ugly beautiful.

Forgiveness means that the cross is our new tree of life from which we are invited to eat. In the fourth century, St John Chrysostom wrote of the cross:

> The Tree is my eternal salvation. It is my nourishment and my banquet. Amidst its roots, I cast my own roots deep. Beneath its boughs I grow. Flying from the burning heart, I have set up my tent in its shadow and have found there a resting place, fresh with dew. I flower with its flowers. Its fruits bring perfect joy, fruits which have been preserved for me since time began, fruits which now I freely eat. This tree is food, sweet food, for my hunger and a fountain for my thirst; it is clothing for my nakedness; its leaves are the breath of life. If I fear God, this is my protection; if I stumble this is my staff; this is the prize for which I fight, the reward of my victory. This is my straight and narrow path; this is Jacob's ladder, where angels go up and down, and where the Lord himself stands at the top.[1]

Forgiveness means that we dare to face what we have done. We dare to remember all of our lives, with the failures and defeats, with our cruelties and lack of love. We dare to remember all the times that we have been mean and ungenerous, the ugliness of our deeds. We dare to remember not so as to feel awful, but so as to open our lives to this creative transformation. It does not leave us as we are, as if nothing we did ever mattered. If we step into that forgiveness, then it will change and transform us. Whatever is sterile and barren will bear fruit. All that is pointless will find meaning. At the end of *Lord of the Rings* Sam scatters around the barren shire the magical fertilizer that the elves have given him, and the next spring every tree blossoms. That is an image of forgiveness.

Jesus asks for forgiveness not just for what they do to him. He is not crucified alone. There are two people on either side. They stand for all the millions of people throughout history whom we have crucified. Think of the Holocaust with which so many Christians were either complicit or else failed to resist. Pope John XXIII prayed:

> We realize that the mark of Cain stands on our foreheads. Across the centuries our brother Abel has lain in blood which we drew or shed tears we

caused forgetting Thy love. Forgive us for the curse we falsely attached to their name as Jews. Forgive us for crucifying Thee a second time in their flesh. For we knew not what we did.[2]

Who are the people whom we crucify now, with our economic imperialism that is producing so much poverty? Who are we crucifying through our violence and war? Whom do we wound even within our own homes? Because we know that forgiveness comes first, then we can dare to open our eyes.

A cross by Michael Finn

This is a cross that was made by a friend of mine, Michael Finn, who is also the father of a friend and brother of mine in St Dominic, Richard. Michael is well known for his abstract paintings but in the last twenty years of his life he created some extraordinarily powerful crucifixes. These were often made with the driftwood that he and his wife Cely found when they walked on the beaches near their home in Cornwall.[3] Michael died on Palm Sunday 2002, the day that Jesus enters Jerusalem to face his own death.

If forgiveness is God's creativity breaking in and transforming us, our ugliness and sterility, then maybe we need artists like Michael to express it best. Beauty is not decorative but makes visible the working of grace in our lives. Simone Weil said that it was sacramental of God's smile. Art can reveal how even that supremely ugly object which is the cross can come to be seen as beautiful. In *The Dream of the Rood* it is described as:

A wondrous Tree towering in the air,
Most shining of crosses compassed with light.
Brightly that beacon was gilded with gold;
Jewels adorned it fair at the foot,
five on the should-beam blazing in splendour.[4]

It is said that Michelangelo found an ugly piece of marble which another artist had been trying to carve but had failed and had ruined the stone. Michelangelo carved out of it his famous David. This is what God's forgiveness does in a way that is beyond our understanding. Forgiveness means that our sins can find their place in our path to God. No failure need be a dead end. And so Augustine spoke of Adam and Eve's sin as a *felix culpa*, a happy fault, because it led to the coming of Christ. When we sin, we commit acts which are fruitless and absurd, and which subvert the meaning of our lives. Forgiveness means that a story can be told which goes somewhere, to happiness.

In the eighteenth century there was a famous Japanese artist called Hokusaï. He painted a vase with a superb view of the holy mountain, Fuji Yama. Then one day someone dropped the vase! Slowly he glued the pieces back together. But to acknowledge what had happened to this vase, its broken history, he lined each join with a thread of gold. The vase was more beautiful than ever before.

1 Taken from a breviary. Multiple versions available.
2 Quoted in Eliezer Berkovits, *Faith after the Holocaust*, New York, 1973, p. 26.
3 Anthony Phillips has used Michael Finn's crosses beautifully to illustrate his meditations on the Seven Last Words, *Entering into the Mind of God*, London, 2002.
4 *Anglo-Saxon Poetry*, trans. and ed. S. A. J. Bradley, London, 1982, p. 160.

The cross of the Lay Fraternity in Norfolk Prison

2. 'Today you will be with me in Paradise.'
Luke 23.43

'Today you will be with me in Paradise.' On Good Friday, two days before he rises from the dead, Jesus makes this astonishing claim that *today* the good thief will be with him in Paradise. So we see that God has a different sense of time that we do. God forgives us before we have even sinned, and Jesus promises to bring this thief into Paradise before he himself has even risen from the dead. This is because God lives in the Today of eternity. God's eternity breaks into our lives now. Eternity is not what happens at the end of time, after we are dead. Every time we love and forgive then we have put a foot into eternity, which is God's life. And that is why we can be joyful even on Good Friday, even in the face of suffering and death.

I remember going to see a Dominican called Gervase Matthew who was dying in hospital. He said to me, 'Timothy, I am about to die. Go and buy two bottles of beer so that we may drink a toast to the Kingdom of God.' So I went weeping to buy the beer from the nearest off-licence. And while we were drinking it a nurse came by and said, 'Father Gervase! You know that you are not allowed alcohol with your pills.' And he replied, 'Don't be silly. I shall die tomorrow morning, and so now I drink to the Kingdom.' When I told Gervase that I must phone to cancel a lecture that I was due to give in London that evening, he told me that he had never stopped anyone from teaching. I must go and give the lecture and he would still be alive when I returned the next day, which he was.

This man says to Jesus, 'Remember me when you come into your Kingdom'. He recognizes that Jesus is a King. What can it mean to accept that this humiliated and powerless man on a cross is a King? What it means is this: Jesus promised us that we will attain happiness, and we will. Human beings are made to be happy and all the powers that threaten our happiness will not prevail. Happiness is not an emotion that we just may or may not have. It is being alive. We will attain our destiny and nothing can stop that because Jesus rules.

We live in a society that is enormously preoccupied by the search for happiness. We live in dread of all that might threaten that happiness: loneliness, the collapse of relationships, failure, poverty, disgrace. Today we rejoice because Jesus says to us too, 'You will be with me in Paradise.' All that we have to do is to accept this gift when it comes.

It never says in the Gospel that the two people on either side are thieves, only that they are wrong doers. But the tradition is wise to call him 'the good thief'. It is a good description. He knows how to get hold of what is not his. He pulls off the most amazing coup in history. He gets Paradise without paying for it. As do we all. We just have to learn how to accept gifts.

I am one of six children, five of them boys. My father was a fanatical cricketer and most of my brothers excelled at the sport. I was the most dismal failure. My father would get us all in a circle and have us throw cricket balls at each other. We had to learn the art of catching. God throws happiness at us all the time. We have to learn to keep our eyes and our hands open so that we can catch it when it comes. We are bombarded with God tossing happiness at us, if we can be quick-eyed enough to spot it.

What is this happiness that Jesus offers? He describes it as Paradise. The word comes from Persian and means 'a walled garden'. The Chinese have an expression, 'If you want to be happy for a week, get married. If you wish to be happy for a month, slaughter a pig. If you wish to be happy for ever, plant a garden.' As a typical Englishman I like that image. But Paradise is more than spending an eternity wandering around the rose bushes.

Mark's Gospel begins with the baptism of Jesus, and when Jesus emerges from the water a voice is heard from heaven proclaiming, 'You are my beloved Son, in whom I delight.' At the heart of the life of the Trinity is this mutual delight of the Father in the Son and the Son in the Father who is the Holy Spirit. Meister Eckhart, the fourteenth-century German Dominican, said, 'The Father laughs at the Son and the Son laughs at the Father, and the laughter brings forth pleasure and the pleasure brings forth joy, and the joy brings forth love.'[1] He describes God's joy as like the exuberance of a horse that gallops around the field, kicking its heels in the air.

The story of the Gospel is of how we are invited to find our home in that happiness. St Catherine of Siena compared it to basking in a big soft bed or the sea. It is God's delight in us and our delight in God. God says to each of us, 'It is wonderful that you exist.' We can be in God's presence with all our weakness and failure, like the good thief, and still God takes pleasure in our very existence and promises Paradise to us.

There is an English film called *Chariots of Fire*, which describes two athletes who train for the Olympics. Their dream is to beat the Americans. One of them, a Scottish Presbyterian called Eric Liddel, says, 'God made me fast and when I run I feel his pleasure in my speed.' God takes pleasure in all that we are. The Church has not a word to say on any moral issues until people have glimpsed God's delight in them. This is the beginning of the good news, that Jesus eats and drinks with the tax collectors and the prostitutes. Until this delight is known, then nothing else can be understood.

This happiness is not incompatible with sorrow. All the most joyful saints were also sorrowful. St Dominic laughed with his brethren in the day and wept at night with God for the sufferings of the world. St Francis was filled with joy, but he bore the stigmata of the cross. When he beheld the seraph on Mount La Verna, 'he was filled with sweetness and sorrow mingled with wonder. Joy he had exceeding great ... but he suffered unspeakable grief and compassion'.[2] Happiness means that we share God's delight in humanity. That means that we must also share God's sorrow at the suffering of his sons and daughters. You cannot have one without the other. Sorrow hollows out our hearts so that there is a space in which God's happiness can dwell.

The opposite of happiness is not sadness. It is being stony hearted. It is refusing to let yourself be touched by other people. It is putting on armour that protects your heart from being moved. If you would be happy then you must be drawn out of yourself and, so, vulnerable. Happiness and true sorrow are ecstatic. They liberate us from ourselves, to take pleasure in other people and to be sorrowed by their pain. The bad thief refuses this. The good thief dares to do this, even on the cross. And that is why he can receive the gift of Paradise.

The cross of the Lay Fraternity in Norfolk Prison

This cross was made by members of the Lay Dominican Fraternity at Norfolk Prison, in Massachusetts. Most of our brothers there are serving long sentences. Some will never obtain parole. During the General Chapter on Rhode Island, on 29 July 2001, I went to spend some time with them. I thought that I would have to cheer them up but they gave me enormous joy. Among the gifts that they gave me was a statue of St Dominic carved out of wax, and this cross made of paper. For reasons of security they are not allowed to use more solid materials.

On this cross they have written their names. We do not know the name of the person to whom Jesus promised Paradise as he hung on the cross. But every day I can see the names of these brothers of mine who endure their own crucifixion. They asked me what might be their vocation as members of the Order of Preachers in this prison. I suggested that they might be preachers of hope. And this is what they are, for those inside and outside the prison. When I left they gave me 200 lovely paper roses, one for each of the members of the General Chapter. That was also a preaching of the gospel, and the sharing of a hope for happiness.

At the top of the cross they have written the motto of the Order 'Truth', and also 'Sing a New Song', the title of my first book. Their presence in that prison is a planting of the gospel truth in a dark place, where they sing a new song far better than I ever could.

1   Sermon 18, in F. Pfeiffer, Aalen, 1962, quoted in Paul Murray, 'Dominicans and Happiness' in *Dominican Ashram*, September 2000, p. 132.
2   Brother Ugolino, *The Little Flowers of St Francis of Assisi*, New York, 1910, p. 114.

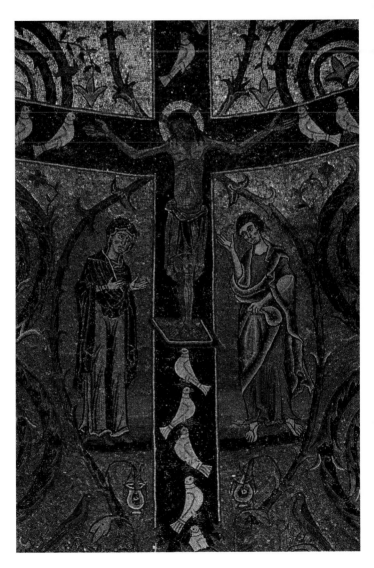

The cross of San Clemente

3. 'Woman, Behold your Son! ... Behold your mother.' John 19.26–27

When Jesus saw his mother, and the disciple whom he loved standing near, he said to his mother, 'Woman, behold your son!' Then he said to the disciple, 'Behold, your mother!' and from that hour the disciple took her to his own home.

Good Friday has seen the disintegration of Jesus' community. Judas has sold him; Peter has denied him, and most of the disciples have run away. All Jesus' labours to build a little community seem to have failed. And then, at the darkest moment, we see this community coming into being at the foot of the cross. His mother is given a son in his closest friend, and the beloved disciple is given a mother.

It is not just any community. It is our community. This is the birth of the Church. He does not call Mary 'Mother'. He says 'Woman'. This is because she is the new Eve. The old Eve was the mother of all living beings. This is the new Eve who is the mother of all who live by faith. So this is our family. Here we see our mother and our brother.

Why is our new family born at the foot of a cross? It is because what breaks up human community is hostility and accusation. We are hostile to other people because they are not like us: they are black or white or Chinese; they are Jewish or Muslim; they are homosexual; they are progressive or conservative. We look at others with accusation and seek to expel them. Societies are often built upon exclusion. We seek scapegoats who can bear away upon their backs our fears and rivalries.

Jesus takes upon himself all our hostility, all the accusations which human beings make against each other. He is 'the stone which the builders rejected which has become the corner stone' (Ps. 119). As James Alison has written, 'God is among us as one cast out.'[1] At the centre of our worship is the one who was expelled. Whom do you accuse today? Whom do you blame for the ills of society, or your own pain?

To be a Christian is to recognize that at the foot of the cross is born our family, from which no one can be excluded. We are brothers and sisters of each other.

This is not just a nice honorary title, like calling a priest 'Father'. In Christ we are kith and kin. We share the same blood, the blood of the cross. The proper way to address another Christian is 'brother' or 'sister'. If you were to start doing that, people would look at you as if you were odd. We are odd! To call someone your brother or sister is not just to state a relationship; it is the proclamation of reconciliation. When Joseph reveals himself to his brothers, he says to them 'I am your brother, Joseph, whom you sold into Egypt' (Genesis 45.4). It is the statement of a healing truth.

In many parts of the world, and especially in the West, our Church is riven by divisions and polarization. Mary and the beloved disciple are brought to the cross by their love of Christ. But their loves are different, that of a mother and that of his closest friend. But there they become one family. There is no competition or rivalry. The New Testament embraces all sorts of utterly different ways of articulating our faith.

Each of us is brought to Christ by a different sort of love. And often we do not recognize our God in the love of another person. We can dismiss their faith as traditional or progressive, as romantic and woolly, or intellectual and abstract. We may see it as a threat which we must deal with by expulsion. But there at the foot of the cross we find each other as family. Imagine if we were to think of Cardinal Ratzinger as our brother Joseph, and Professor Küng as Brother Hans, and Mother Angelica as our sister. We are given the task of reaching across all the boundaries and hostilities that divide human beings and saying 'Behold my brother', 'Behold my sister'.

When war with Iraq began to loom, the Dominican Leadership Conference of the United States issued bumper stickers that said 'We have family in Iraq'. Of course they were thinking in the first place of our Dominican brothers and sisters, of brethren in Baghdad and Mossul, and of our sisters who are in most parts of the country. They thought also that all Iraqis *are* our brothers and sisters, children of Abraham, regardless of whether they are Muslim or Christian.

Archbishop Helder Camara of Recife, in Brazil, had a deep sense that the very poorest people were his family. If he heard that one had been unjustly arrested, then he would telephone the police and say, 'I hear that you have arrested my brother.' And the police would become very apologetic. 'Your excellency, we are so sorry. We did not know he was your brother. Please come and collect him.' And when the Archbishop would go to the police station to collect the man, the police might say, 'But your Excellency, he does not have the same family name as you.' And Camara would reply that every poor person was his brother and sister.

Finally, what about our ordinary families, the parents who gave us life, the people we marry and the children we beget? A Christian family propels us beyond its boundaries. It turns us outwards to discover other brothers and sisters who are not relatives. Jesus says to Mary, 'Behold your son.' Open your eyes. See, this person is your son. Christian parents can follow that example. You can say to your children, 'Open your eyes and see. This stranger, this Iraqi, this Russian, this Jew, this Muslim is your brother or sister.' A family should form us to belong to humanity.

A good friend of mine is a Dominican sister who belongs to a vast family or some ten or eleven siblings. Every Christmas they gather together for a party. One day she noticed a couple of people whom she did not recognize. She went up and asked them how they were related. And they replied that they had just been driving by, had seen this wonderful party and so they just wandered in. And they stayed.

The cross of San Clemente

Earlier this year I visited Austin Flannery, an Irish Dominican. I noticed on his desk a beautiful reproduction of the mosaic cross in the apse of the Basilica of San Clemente in Rome, which was given to the Irish Dominicans in 1677. It was a base for the Irish Province during the time of persecution when it was not possible for the brethren to live together openly in their own country. When I admired this cross Austin immediately gave it to me, so I value it above all as a sign of friendship. St Thomas understands the love which is the life of the Trinity in terms of friendship. So we are called to find our home in God's own friendship and find God in all our friendships.

The cross also suggests how large is our home. On either side of the cross are Mary and the Beloved Disciple, John. The cross has twelve doves on it. I assume that these represent the twelve apostles who will be filled with the Holy Spirit at Pentecost and sent to the ends of the world. So, even at this darkest moment one sees in embryo the vast communion of the Church. The cross is not just an instrument of torture. The outreach of its arms helps us to understand 'what is the breadth and length and height and depth' (Ephesians 3.18) of God's love.

The Basilica itself shows that this communion stretches not just across present divisions between human beings but also across time. In 1857 an Irish Dominican called Mullooly began to excavate beneath the Basilica and he discovered the remains of a fourth-century church, which one can still visit. The cross that we see was probably copied from the mosaics of that first church, one of the earliest in Rome. In fact some of the *tesserae* may date from the fourth century. If so, then the image that we see spans eight centuries in its making. And below the fourth century church were discovered the remains of a first-century Mithraic temple. So San Clemente and this cross suggest the vast span of the community that was born beneath Christ's cross, embracing saints and sinners, the living and the dead, and stretching out for the whole of humanity.

1 *Knowing Jesus*, London, 1993, p. 71.

A cross from Haiti

4. 'My God, my God, why have you forsaken me?'
Mark 15.34

At midday a darkness fell over the whole land, which lasted till three in the afternoon; and at three Jesus cried aloud, 'Eloi, Eloi, lema sabach-tani?' which means, 'My God, my God, why have you forsaken me?'

The first three sayings of Jesus have shown how even in this darkest moment something is hatching here. They have shown us forgiveness, happiness and the birth of community. But here, at the turning point of our reflections, are these words of pure desolation. Here we just have a cry of pain and loneliness. Is it a question without an answer? Is there anything to be said at all?

In his black hole under Beirut, Brian Keenan felt 'bereft of God'. This is more than doubting God's existence, as one might doubt whether some historical character ever lived. It is more than the absence of someone whom one loves. It is the collapse of all meaning, as if the pith and centre of one's life had been sucked out and one was left hovering over a void. He wrote:

> I am full with nothing. My prayers rebound on me as if all those words that I sent up were poured back upon me like an avalanche tumbling around me. I am bereft even of God. My own words become bricks and stones that bruise me. I have been lifted up and emptied out. I am a bag of flesh and scrape, a heap of offal tossed unwanted in the corner of this filthy room.[1]

Few of us will ever have endured such utter desolation, but there may have been moments when we feared to be swallowed by the void, and when our lives appeared to be without sense or meaning, because God had gone. In such times proofs of the existence of God are no great help. Words do not help much.

These terrible words of Jesus are a quotation from Psalm 22. Someone several hundred years earlier had been in anguish and he or she wrote these words down. Now Jesus takes these words and he makes them his own. He embraces that experience of desolation and shares it. Even the experience of the absence of God is somehow brought within God's own life.

Elie Wiesel has written about the terrible hangings that he witnessed when he was in Auschwitz during the Second World War. The worst was when they hanged two adults and a young boy, who was everyone's favorite. Everyone was lined up to witness the deaths.

> The three victims mounted together on to the chairs. The three necks were placed at the same moment within the nooses. 'Long live liberty' cried the adults. But the child was silent. 'Where is God? Where is He?' someone behind me asked. At a sign from the head of the camp, the three chairs tipped over. Total silence throughout the camp. On the horizon the sun was setting. Then the march past began. The two adults were no longer alive. Their tongues hung swollen, blue-tinged. But the third rope was still moving; being so light the child was still alive ... For more than half an hour he stayed there, struggling between life and death, dying in slow agony under our eyes. And we had to look him full in the face. He was still alive when I passed in front of him. His tongue was still red; his eyes were not yet glazed. Behind me, I heard the same man asking: 'Where is God now?' And I heard a voice within me answer him: 'Where is He? He is – He is hanging here on this gallows.'[2]

Sometimes we must be with people who are faced with a suffering that appears pointless, absurd and meaningless. We may live such moments ourselves. Someone we love may be faced with death by cancer when they are in the prime of life, or we may lose a child in an accident. We may suddenly find our lives ruined and senseless. At this particular moment we share in the anguish of death in Iraq. Someone may ask us: 'Why? Why? Where is God now?' And we may be terrified by finding that we have nothing to say. All the pious words that come to our lips sound worse than empty. Then all that we can do is to be there, and trust that God is there too.

Primo Levi, an Italian Jew, was also in Auschwitz. He recounts how one day he was going crazy with thirst and he saw a beautiful icicle. He reached out to grab it and suck it, but he was stopped by the guard. So Levi said 'Warum?' 'Why?' And the guard replied, 'Hier is kein warum?' 'Here there is no "Why?".'[3] We may all live through moments that are absurd, where there is no why or wherefore. Then we cannot seek for easy answers. It would be blasphemous to offer explanations. All we can do is trust that God is here.

I was in Rwanda when a terrible violence broke out. That day I was due to drive to the north to visit our Dominican sisters working in the refugee camps. The Belgian Ambassador came and told us not to go. It was too dangerous. But we negotiated our way past the roadblock at the edge of the city of Kigali and we drove north. Several times our car was stopped, by soldiers or by rebels, and we had to get out. I remember masked men with swords and guns hauling us out of the car, and I thought that the end had come. We got through each time. We saw the utter misery of the refugee camps. We visited a prison that was like an abattoir. We went to a hospital filled with children who had lost their limbs through mines. I remember one child who had lost both legs, one arm and an eye. They had no money to buy crutches, let alone artificial limbs, and so they had to hop. And I went outside into the bush and I wept.

That evening we celebrated the Eucharist in the sitting room of the sisters. The walls were filled with bullet holes from the recent fighting. When the time came to preach a little sermon, I had no words for all that I had seen. I had never met such suffering before. Anything that I could say seemed trite, banal. But I did not have to say anything. I was given something to do, a ritual to perform. We re-enacted what Jesus did on the night before he died. We repeated his words, 'This is my body, given for you.'

When we utter words of utter anguish, then we remember that on the cross Jesus made them his own. And when we can find no words at all, not even to scream, then we may take his.

A cross from Haiti

This cross was painted by a peasant from our parish in the western mountains of Haiti, one of the poorest countries in the world. For years the people suffered under a ruthless dictatorship. If anyone opposed in any way that tyranny, then they would be taken away. Usually their bodies were found a few days later in a ditch. When a body was discovered, one of the brethren would go to photograph it so that there would be some record and the memory of the murder would not be lost. When I first visited the country, there was a new government and some form of democracy had returned, but the poverty was still immense.

On this cross there is a path which weaves its way up the central column. We do not see the end of the journey, but trust that there is one. On it walks a peasant with his back to us. On that cross was nailed the one who is called in their Creole *Bondié Pitit*, 'The Little One of the Good God'. The peasant is alone and we presume silent. Most Haitians are still walking that path of suffering. And yet along that path all sorts of exotic plants grow, and it leads to a tall palm tree with long fronds, a sign of hope. And beyond the hills we can see the first signs of dawn.

This is the cross I always take with me when I travel, together with a small icon of Our Lady and the child Jesus, from the beginning and end of Jesus' life. It has got a little dirty, and sometimes I have had to glue it together again when it has been broken. The gospel says that one must daily take up one's cross and follow Jesus. That sounds rather gloomy, but this is a cross that I have been happy to take up on my travels. If one travels a lot, then one needs signs of continuity, of a home remade on the journey. And so this peasant on his path travels with me, and I hope that in some small way I with him.

1   *An Evil Cradling*, p. 67.
2   *Night*, ET, London, 1960, pp. 76f.
3   *If this is a Man: The Truce*, London, 1965, p. 35.

A cross from El Salvador

5. 'I thirst.'
John 19.28

After this Jesus, knowing that all was now finished, said (to fulfill the scripture), 'I thirst.'

Right at the beginning of John's Gospel, Jesus met the Samaritan woman at the well and he said to her, 'Give me water.' At the beginning and the end of the story Jesus asks us to satisfy his thirst. This is how God comes to us, in a thirsty person wanting something that we have to give. God's relationship with creation is entirely that of gift. To be a creature is to receive one's being as a gift. God wishes to be in friendship with us, and friendship always implies equality. And so the one who gives us everything invites us into friendship by asking for a gift back, whatever we may have to give. The Chief Rabbi, Jonathan Sacks, explains that according to the Jewish tradition we should not only give to the poor, we should enable them also to give to others. It belongs to their dignity to be not only recipients but also givers. There is an African proverb that the hand that gives is always uppermost and the hand that receives is lower down. God makes friendship with us by coming to us as one who begs for what we have.

Most of all he wants us. Usually we think that reaching God is hard work. We must earn forgiveness; we must become good, otherwise he will disapprove of us. But this is wrong. God comes to us before we have ever turned to him. God thirsts for our love. He is racked with desire for us. As the fourteenth-century mystic Julian of Norwich wrote:

The same desire and thirst that he had upon the cross (which desire, longing and thirst, as to my sight, was in him from without beginning) the same hath he yet, and shall have unto the time that the last soul that shall be saved is come up into his bliss. For as verily as there is a property in God of truth and pity, so verily there is a property in God of thirst and longing ... which is lasting in him as long as we be in need, drawing us up to his blessing ... The longing and the ghostly thirst of Christ lasteth and shall last until Doomsday.[1]

There is something very embarrassing about admitting that you long for someone when the other person does not fully reciprocate. One feels foolish and vulnerable admitting that one loves more than one is loved. The moment that we own up to our longing, then we become open to rejection and humiliation. Yet this is how it is with God. God is overwhelmed with thirst for us and for our love, and yet he must put up with the occasional rather condescending pat on the head. 'Oh it's Sunday, we had better go and visit God', as if God were a boring relative. So when we find ourselves more loving than loved, then we are in God's position. As C. S. Lewis said, 'It is a divine privilege always to be less the beloved than the lover.'[2] Then we may dare to say, with the poet Auden:

If equal affection cannot be,
Let the more loving one be me.[3]

We are thirsty too. The medievals thought of Christ on the cross as trampling the grapes that would make the wine that would satisfy our thirst. Just as at Cana he had turned water into wine, so on the cross he makes his blood the wine of eternal life. In the last of the 'fifteen Oes of St Bridget', there is the prayer: 'O Jesu, true and fruitful vine, remember the overflowing and abundant out-pouring of your blood, which you shed copiously, as though squeezed from a cluster of grapes, when on the Cross you trod the wine-press alone.'[4]

Maybe we do not really thirst for God as yet. Maybe we only have little thirsts: for ordinary good Napa Valley red rather than the wine of the Kingdom, for a bit more money, for companionship, for success at work. If these are our little desires, then we must start there. The Samaritan woman wanted water and so she went to the well and there met Jesus. If we are honest about our little desires, then they will lead us to Jesus too. We will learn to become thirsty for more, even to become thirsty for God who thirsts for us. Most people think of religion as about the control of desire. Desire is dangerous and disturbing and so religion helps us tame it. But traditionally this has not been the teaching of the Church. We are invited to deepen our desires, to touch their hidden hunger, to liberate desire in recognition of its ultimate goal.

Thirst is a very fundamental experience. I have only been really thirsty once, walking with my brethren in the desert heat from Jerusalem to Jericho. After a while we began to feel disorientated, almost disembodied. One of our companions did go slightly crazy with thirst but for those who face suffering it is often the climax of their trials.

Brian Keenan, in his hell hole in Beirut, longs for words and for water:

I must ration my drinking water for I am always fearful that I might finish it and then wake in the middle of the night with a raging thirst that I cannot satiate. I think of rabies and the raging thirst of mad dogs and I know how easy it would be to go mad from thirst. Now I know the full meaning of the expression so frequently used in our daily lives: 'He was mad with thirst.'

And another time, when he is with his companion John McCarthy, one of the guards ask him what he wants:

'Water, give me some water,' I answered, angry, not caring that they should know my anger. They gave me a bottle of water. I gulped it down, almost choking myself with another huge swallow of water. 'John,' I said again, 'here, drink.' I handed the bottle to him. One of the guards again asked 'Do you want anything?' and I answered with loud sarcasm 'Yes, I want a swimming pool!' I wanted to defuse myself in cool, clear, crisp water. I wanted to feel my body languidly move through it, to be alone and free in the vast sunlight with cool water caressing my flesh.[5]

If it does not seem absurd to mention this terrible lived suffering with a fiction, I cannot but note that thirst is the climax of the most popular myth of our time, *Lord of the Rings*. At the end of long trek of Frodo and Sam, the final test, as they climb the mountain to destroy the ring, the ultimate challenge is thirst.

At their last halt Frodo sank down and said, 'I am thirsty, Sam', and did not speak again. Sam gave him a mouthful of water, only one more mouthful remained. He went without himself; and now as once more the night of Mordor closed over them, through all his thoughts there came the memory of water; and every brook or stream or fount that he had ever seen, under green willow-shades or twinkling in the sun, danced and rippled for his torment behind the blindness of his eyes.[6]

Why is it that thirst for water is so fundamental? Maybe it is because our bodies are 98 per cent water. Dehydration is the seeping away of our very being, our substance. We feel that we ourselves are evaporating. So often the last desire of those who are dying is for something to drink. It also stands for that deepest thirst for the one who gives us substance and being at every moment and who promises eternal life: 'Oh God, you are my God for you I long; for you my soul is thirsting. My body pines for you, like a dry weary land without water' (Psalm 62).

A cross from El Salvador

This cross was a gift that I received in El Salvador and is typical of the country. During my first visit to the Province of Central America, I had a meeting with the novices and each one of them presented me with a gift, something that he had made himself: a painting, a poem, a song, a cross, a pot, or whatever. There was no artistic snobbery. It belongs to the ordinary life of men and women that they should be creative. If the gift is to represent you, then it is right that it be your own work. When I travelled around the Order, I was presented with endless gifts, and it was of the profoundest importance to receive them with gratitude, even if sometimes I could not imagine how to carry them all. I once arrived in Vietnam with 8 kilos of luggage, and left with 65 kilos!

On the cross, the dying Christ asks for the gift of water. But in a moment he will die and his side will be opened, and out will pour living water. He will unlock our own fertility. As he said in the Temple, 'If anyone thirst, let him come to me and drink. He who believes in me, as the scripture has said, "Out of his heart shall flow rivers of living water"' (John 7.37f.).

This little cross shows us the fertility of the cross, with its fruit and flowers, and a multicoloured cow and rabbit. At its centre, where Christ's body was, is the woman, to whose fertility we each owe our existence, and often so neglected by the Church. May the Body of Christ be nourished by the wisdom and creativity of women.

1 *Revelations of Divine Love*, ed. Dom Roger Hudleston, London, 1927, p. 76.
2 *Four Loves*, London, 1960, p. 184.
3 'The More Loving One', *Collected Shorter Poems*, p. 282.
4 Eamon Duffy, *The Stripping of the Altars*, p. 252.
5 *An Evil Cradling*, pp. 63, 216.
6 *The Return of the King*, Book Six, 'Mount Doom' (multiple editions).

The rosary cross

6. 'It is finished.'
John 19.30

A bowl full of vinegar stood there; so they put a sponge full of the vinegar
on hyssop and held it to his mouth. When Jesus had received the vinegar,
he said, 'It is finished', and he bowed his head and gave up his spirit.

'It is finished.' Jesus' cry does not just mean that it is all over and that he will
now die. It is a cry of triumph. It means, 'It is completed.' What he literally says
is, 'It is perfected.' At the beginning of the Last Supper, St John tells us that
'having loved his own who were in the world, he loved them to perfection'. On
the cross we see the perfection of love.

I hope that we have all been touched by dreams of perfect love, love that is
utter and complete. When we are young, we become infatuated and we may
think that no one has ever been so totally in love as us. At least I did! I remember
falling head over heels in love with a cousin of mine at a dance when I was 16. I
carried her off the dance floor in ecstasy, and rather absurdly. Later I found her
kissing someone else in the bushes. That was *not* why I joined the Dominicans!

When people marry, then usually they are more mature than I was then, but
often there is still the dream of the perfection of love. No matter what anyone
may say, many people marry feeling sure that they are at the beginning of eternal bliss. And when I joined the Order, as a rather innocent twenty-year-old, I
was sure that I would love God and the brethren utterly and forever. The honey-
moon would never end.

It does. One soon discovers that one's love is not so perfect. One has not been
transformed, and remains much the same selfish, self-centred person as before.
And the beloved also may come to seem not quite so fantastic either. He or she
may be self-centred, have a terrible sense of humour, snore in bed, or have other
irritating habits. Was that dream of perfect love just an illusion? Do we become
cynical?

These words of Jesus invite us to carry on seeking to love perfectly. We will
arrive at that fullness of love in the end and at the end. In fact each of these
sayings of Jesus shows us the successive steps in the deepening expression of

his love for us. 'Forgive them for they know not what they do.' In these words he does not even address us. He talks to his Father. 'Today you will be with me in Paradise.' This is a more intimate love. It is addressed to us, but from above, as a king. 'Behold your mother. Behold your Son.' This is a further step towards closeness, addressed to us not as a king but as our brother. 'My God, my God, why have you forsaken me?' This is so deeply intimate that he has entered into our very souls and embraced our own desolation. But the perfection of love is in the words, 'I thirst.' The fullness of love is when Jesus begs for something from us and accepts it with gratitude. Now his love is complete.

The soldiers give Jesus what they have, some sour old vinegar. It probably tasted disgusting but it is what poor soldiers drank and so they shared it. They could not afford decent wine. Jesus accepts what they have to offer. At the feeding of the five thousand, Jesus asked the disciples what they had to give to the crowd, and they reply, 'Just five loaves and two fish.' It is not much. It is all that they have and so it is enough. Faced with our hungry world, with millions who are starving, we may not feel that we have much to give. If we give what we have, then it will be enough.

The perfection of love is when we receive the gift of the other person as he or she is. They may not be quite what we had dreamed of. They may be less intelligent, less witty than we hoped. They will certainly one day be less beautiful. We dreamed of first-growth claret and what we got may just be old vinegar. If we can accept that gift with gratitude, then our love will be on the way to perfection.

The film *Love Actually* begins and ends in the arrivals hall of Heathrow airport. We hear Hugh Grant assuring us that if we open our eyes then we shall see that love is all around us. It may not always be heroic or romantic or between beautiful people. It may be dumb and fumbling for a voice. It comes in all sorts of odd forms, between people of different generations, of different or the same sex. But where it is, then God is present.

Perfect love is possible and we see it on the cross. If we love at all, then God's perfect love can make its home in our fragile and faulted loves. St Augustine writes, 'You have begun to love? God has begun to dwell in you.'[1] If we accept to love the other person as they are, without complaint or blame, then God's perfect love will make its home in us.

The rosary cross

This is the cross on a rosary made by the Dominican nuns of the monastery in Catamarca, Argentina. It was brought by the Provincial of Argentina to the General Chapter in 1992, in Mexico, to be given to whom ever was elected Master of the Order, as a sign of their prayers and their love. So it was not a gift that was intended for me personally. I just happened to be the person elected. One might think that would make it less significant. How could they promise to love this unknown person? I detest those automatic messages in car parks and shops that assure you that you are a deeply significant person whose custom is so valued. Empty words.

And yet this pledge by the nuns does have a deeply Christian significance. We are commanded to love our neighbour as ourself. We do not know who that neighbour will be or whether he or she will be obviously loveable. Yet there is a fundamental trust that since they are created by God then they are indeed loveable, if we can but see them with God's eyes, who loves all that he has made. The gift of this rosary expresses a belief in the Creator, who sees that what he has made is very good. St Augustine wrote right at the end of the *Confessions*: 'All these works of yours we see. We see that together they are very good, because it is you who see them in us and it was you who gave us the Spirit by which we see them and love you in them.'[2]

To see the goodness of another person often requires a certain repose. We must be with them, unhurriedly, wasting time with them. If we are rushing then we are more likely to see them in functional terms, as useful or as hindering our projects. The perfection of love implies leisure, in which one can be receptive to another, almost passively attentive.

During my years of travel, that was a leisure that I rarely knew. Masters of the Order have always complained that they were too busy to pray. Raymond of Peñafort wrote to the Prioress of Bologna that he was so occupied at the papal court, that 'I am hardly ever able to reach or, to be quite honest, even to see from afar the tranquility of contemplation ... So it is a great joy and an enormous comfort to me to know that I am helped by your prayers.'[3] Jordan of Saxony, Dominic's immediate successor, writes to his beloved Diana, 'Pray for me often and earnestly in the Lord; I am much in need of prayer because of my faults, and I pray but seldom myself.'[4] During my years as Master I travelled for up to eight months a year, usually sleeping in a different bed each night. There was little time just to be still. As with Jack Aubrey on HMS *Surprise*, there was never a moment to lose. I remember my shame when a friend of mine remarked during a conversation in Mexico that I had looked at my watch twice since we began to talk. The gift of this rosary was a reminder that these contemplative nuns in Argentina were enjoying a deeper peace than I was, I hoped, and that I was remembered in their prayers. It was a promise and a memory of the necessary moments of silence, if our eyes are to be open to recognize and love the goodness of others.

In 2003 Tate Britain celebrated Christmas with an aspen tree decorated with 500 rosaries. This was a welcome improvement on the previous upside-down fir and rubbish bin. This Christmas tree reminds us that, as its creator Mark Wallinger said, 'We only celebrate Christ's birth in the knowledge of the manner of his death.' According to one tradition, the cross was made of aspen. The recitation of the mysteries of the rosary takes us through the narrative of Christ's life from Bethlehem to the empty tomb. It carries one along the journey. So it is somehow fitting that tradition maintains that Our Lady gave the rosary to Dominic, the wandering preacher. It is a good gift from our contemplative nuns to a traveller. It is a way of prayer that offers moments of stillness even when one is on the road.

1 In 1. Jn. 8.
2 XIII. 34.
3 *Early Dominicans: Selected Writings*, ed. Simon Tugwell, OP, New York, 1982, p. 409.
4 Ibid. Letter 25, p. 104.

The Aids pietà

7. 'Father, into your hands I commend my spirit.'
Luke 23.46

It was now about the sixth hour, and there was darkness over the whole
land until the ninth hour, while the sun's light failed, and the curtain of
the Temple was torn in two. Then Jesus, crying with a loud voice, said,
'Father, into thy hands I commend my spirit.'

The first and the last of the seven words are addressed to the Father. The fourth
and central word, the turning point, is as well, but in God's apparent absence.
In the meantime he has addressed us with increasing intimacy: as a king, as a
brother, and as a beggar. Now he gives everything back to the Father. He
entrusts us all, with all our fears and hopes, back into God's hands. It is the
supreme act of trust.

We live in an age of profound anxiety. We are fearful about disease and illness, about our futures, about our children, about our jobs, about failure, about
death. We suffer from a deep insecurity, a collapse of trust. This is strange
because we are far more protected and safe than any previous generation of
human history, at least in the West. We have better medicine, safer transport;
we are more protected from the climate, have better social security. And yet we
are more afraid.

I spent nine years as Master of the Order travelling around the world in
many dangerous places. I saw civil war and genocide in Africa, thousands of
people with leprosy, the signs of endless violence. But when I came back to the
West, I found people who appeared to be more afraid than anywhere else.
September 11 deepened that sense of anxiety. I was in Berkeley, California, when
those few anthrax envelopes were sent and the panic was tangible. But we have
no need for fear. Jesus has entrusted us into the hands of the Father.

I suspect that this pervasive anxiety derives from the fact that we have a culture
of control. We can control so many things: fertility and birth, so much disease
can be cured; we can control the forces of nature; we mine the earth and dam
the rivers. And we westerners control most of humanity. But control is never
complete. We are increasingly aware that our planet may be careering towards

disaster. We live in what Anthony Giddens has called 'a runaway world'.

We are afraid, above all, of death, which unmasks our ultimate lack of control. In *A Single Man*, by Christopher Isherwood, a middle-aged man looks at himself in the mirror:

> Staring, and staring into the mirror, it sees many faces within its face – the face of the child, the boy, the young man, the not-so-young man – all present still, preserved like fossils on superimposed layers, and, like fossils, dead. Their message to this live dying creature is: Look at us – we have died – what is there to be afraid of? It answers them: But that happened so gradually, so easily. *I'm afraid of being rushed.*[1]

A friend of mine had a sign in his room which said, 'Don't worry. It might not happen.' I composed another for him which said, 'Don't worry. It probably will happen. But it won't be the end of the world.' It will not be the end of the world because the world has already ended. When Jesus dies the sun and the moon are darkened; the tombs are opened, and the dead walk. This is the end of which the prophets spoke. The worst that one can ever imagine has already happened. The world collapsed. And then there was Easter Sunday.

Take a moment to think of all that you most fear. For me might it be the shame of public humiliation? Or loneliness? Or a painful death? Or seeing the early death of someone that you love? We can take every possible precaution to avoid these disasters. We can take out all the insurance policies in the world, live healthy lives, go to the gym, and never catch airplanes, have check ups and give up smoking. But what we most fear may still happen. Jesus invites us not to be afraid. All that we dread happened to him on Good Friday, the day that the old world ended and a new world began.

'On the seventh day God finished his work which he had done, and he rested on the seventh day from all his work which he had done' (Genesis 2.2). The rabbis were puzzled by the fact that God finished working on the seventh day but it is not said what he made on that day. And it was concluded that he made rest itself. 'What was created on the 7th day? Tranquility, serenity, peace and repose.'[2] Rest was the goal and completion of creation.

So now Jesus has spoken his seven words, which are leading to the new creation of Easter Sunday. And then he rests. God created us so that we might share that rest, and so that God may rest in us. We are made to rest in God and for

God to rest in us. That rest is not the absence of activity; it is a homecoming. 'If a person loves me, he will keep my word, and my Father will love him, and we will come to him and make our home with him' (John 14.23).

Ambrose of Milan saw Jesus' resting on the cross as a completion of God's rest on the seventh day of Creation. He now rests in us after the labour of his passion. In his commentary on the Six Days of Creation he wrote:

> The sixth day is now completed; the sum of the work of the world has been concluded. Humanity has been created, humanity who rules over every living thing, humanity who is the summing up of the whole universe, humanity who is the delight of every creature in the world. Surely it is time now for us to make our contribution of silence, for now God rests from his work of making the world. He has found rest in the deep places of humanity, in humanity's mind and will and purpose, for he made humanity with the power of reason, he made humanity to imitate himself, to strive after virtue, to be eager for the grace of heaven. God finds comfort here, as he himself witnesses when he says, 'In whom shall I find rest other than in him who is humble and peaceful and who is filled with awe at my words?' I give thanks to the Lord our God who has made a work of such a kind that he could find rest in it. He made the heavens, but I do not read that he then rested. He made the earth, but I do not read that then he rested. He made the sun and the moon and the stars, but I do not read that he found rest there. What I do read is this: he made humanity, and then he found rest in one whose sins he would be able to forgive.
>
> So he has given us a symbolic picture of the passion of the Lord that still lay in the future. He has revealed to us how Christ would one day find his rest in humanity. He has anticipated for himself that sleep of bodily death which he would one day take in order to redeem humanity. Listen again to what he says: 'I sleep and take my rest and I rise up again, for it is the Lord who protects me.' He, the Creator, rested. To him be honour and praise and glory everlasting, glory from the beginning of time, glory now, glory always, glory for ever. Amen.[3]

The Aids pietà

In Britain in the early 1980s we first began to be aware of a new illness, Aids. Some Dominicans of the English Province began to reflect upon how the Church might respond. Especially in those days, Aids victims often suffered from exclusion and isolation. One young man dying in hospital had to drag himself out of bed to get his food since no one would dare to bring it into his room. It seemed to us that the welcome that the victims of Aids received from the Church was a test of our faithfulness to the gospel. One small initiative was the commissioning of this icon by Frances Meigh. In the original Pietà of Michelangelo, the dead Jesus rests finally in the arms of his mother. Here the young man with Aids is still alive, resting in the arms of Jesus who has overcome death. In the background one can see the cross upon which Jesus was stretched out, opening his arms to all those who are expelled. For the Body of Christ has Aids.

This young man rests, at ease and at home. He has no more need than the rest of us to justify his presence. Until he is at home, then none of the rest of us may be fully so. In May 2003 I visited an Aids hospice in Phnom Penh, Cambodia. It is run by an American priest, Jim. It was a simple structure, with a balcony open on the back onto the rice paddies, being worked by water buffaloes. People who could no longer be cared for at home, or who were found ill on the street, were brought there. Some got back a little strength and could go home, if they had one. Most came here to die. There was a young man there who was almost a skeleton. His hair was being tenderly cut and washed. He looked completely at peace. One might wonder whether the care of this one young man could make any difference. Thousands of people with Aids were still left to die on the streets of the city. But it is a sign of that homecoming which is promised to us all. In this Icon Jesus looks at us and invites us to share his peace too.

1 *A Single Man*, London, 1964, p. 8.
2 Abraham Joshua Heschel, *The Sabbath*, New York, 1951, p. 21.
3 Hexaemeron, ix, IQ, 75–76.

Afterword

Beyond Silence

Now Jesus has spoken his last word on the cross. There is silence. We must wait for the resurrection to break the silence of the tomb. God always wishes us to wait for his word. God promised an heir to Abraham and Sarah, but they had to wait for tens of years for the conception of Isaac. God promised the Messiah to his people, but they had to wait thousands of years. God always takes time to speak.

This waiting is hard for us who belong to the Now Generation. We are impatient of delay. On the Internet communication is almost instantaneous. As Zymunt Bauman has written, we have taken 'the waiting out of wanting.'[1] I own up to being a modern man, not in the cuddly Beckham way, but as profoundly impatient, though I have learned to slow down a little, spending much of nine years waiting in airports. One day in Abidjan I was told that a plane was late. 'How late?' 'Three days late.'

'Why are we waiting?' as we used to sing. The Word of God comes as a gift. It cannot be grabbed at. We cannot make it our possession and master it. The Word comes like a person, which indeed it is. We owe it the courtesy of patient attentiveness, letting it come when it wills. Simone Weil wrote that 'we do not obtain the most precious gifts by going in search of them but by waiting for them ... This way of looking is, in the first place, attentive. The soul empties itself of all its own contents in order to receive the human being it is looking at, just as he is, in all his truth ...'[2] Just as one must give someone the space in which to show who they are, so we must give God the space in which to grant that Word, attentive in the silence of Holy Saturday. It comes, as Yann Martel writes in *The Life of Pi* with 'no thundering from a pulpit, no condemnation from bad churches, no peer pressure, just a book of scriptures quietly waiting to say hello, as gentle and powerful as a little girl's kiss on your cheek.'[3]

We must wait for the Word in silence because it erupts from within human language. God is not a very powerful invisible person, who may come storming in from outside, like a celestial superman or a Universal President Bush. We cannot imagine what it meant for Jesus to be raised from the dead, but presumably it was not an external event, but the welling up from Jesus' deepest interiority of his life with the Father. So the Word does not come from outside but gestates within our human language. The Word of God does not come down from heaven like a celestial Esperanto. It takes time to fertilize human language with the Word of God. Pregnancy takes time.

It needed thousands of years for there to be a language in which the Word of God could be spoken at all. Prophets, scribes, lawyers, courtiers and ordinary men and women had to wrestle in attentiveness to God to form a language in which Jesus could speak the words of eternal life. Experiences of exile and liberation, of the rise and fall of kingdoms, the evolution of new notions of law and love, borrowing from the wisdom of Egyptians and Assyrians, the myths of Canaanites and Babylonians, all these were necessary for the language to be ready for the Word to dwell among us.

So now there must be silence as we wait for the giving of the Word that breaks the silence. Even formulation of these Seven Last Words of Jesus took decades. The first Gospel was probably not written until forty years after the Resurrection and the last Gospel maybe another twenty or thirty years after that. Mark's community lived through an acute crisis of waiting in the early seventies in Rome. The apostles were dying, the Church was being persecuted, Christians were betraying each other and falling away and still Jesus did not come. Would he ever come? Have we placed our hope in his words in vain? But Jesus did not come with trumpet blasts, like the cavalry coming to our rescue. He came from within our language in the writing of Matthew, Mark, Luke and John. He irrupted in new words of grace and truth. The Church had to endure prolonged pregnancy before the words were given.

This waiting for the Word requires of us silence and attentiveness, but also sometimes a hard mental struggle. We must learn to be vacant, but that is not enough. We also have to grapple and wrestle to receive the Word that is given now. Annie Dillard captures well the combination of gift and hard grind that is involved the receiving of the Word:

At its best, the sensation of writing is that of any unmerited grace. It is handed to you, but only if you look for it. You search, you break your heart, your back, your brain and then – and only then – it is handed to you. From the corner of your eye you can see motion. Something is moving the air and headed your way.[4]

As one awaits the Word that God will give, one must be quiet, open to what cannot be anticipated, but there is also persistent hard work. Thoreau said of writing, 'Know your own bone; gnaw at it, bury it, unearth it, and gnaw at it still.' That is also part of the waiting.

One of my brethren, a rugged Scot called Anthony Ross, was a famous preacher until he was struck down by a stroke that left him wordless. The specialist who came to see him told him that he would never be able to utter a word again, to which he replied, 'Thank you, doctor.' That left the doctor speechless! Anthony could never say much again, but every word that he struggled to bring out was the fruit of that awful suffering and victory. People would come hundreds of miles to confess to him, waiting for the few words that he would give them. You had to wait for it. Before I left for Rome he gave me a single word, 'Courage'. And it was food for me for a long time. Similarly God's Word takes time to gestate within us.

For us, too, it is often Holy Saturday. As we face war in Iraq, terrorism, starvation in many countries, the explosion of Aids, and all our own personal sufferings, then like the disciples we learn patience as we await a fresh Word, which may be coming to birth. George Steiner ends *Real Presences* thus:

> But ours is the long day's journey of the Saturday. Between suffering, aloneness, unutterable waste on the one hand and the dream of liberation, of rebirth on the other. In the face of the torture of a child, the death of love which is Friday, even the greatest art and poetry are almost helpless. In the Utopia of the Sunday, the aesthetic will, presumably, no longer have logic or necessity. The apprehensions and figurations in the play of metaphysical imagining, in the poem and the music, which tell of pain and of hope, of the flesh which is said to taste of ash and of the spirit which is said to have the savour of fire, are always Sabbatarian. They have risen out of an immensity of waiting which is that of man. Without them, how could we be patient? [5]

As we wait, we look on the dead face of Christ. Although we have been meditating on the Seven Last Words of the still living Christ, none of our crosses have shown him alive. Either he is dead, as in the cross of Michael Finn, or absent as on the crosses from the fraternity of Norfolk Prison, Haiti, El Salvador or the Argentinean rosary. It is only in the Aids pietà that Jesus is alive and looking at us, and there he is not on the cross. It took four hundred years to represent Christ on the cross at all, which can be seen on the doors of Santa Sabina, where I lived in Rome, and a further five hundred to dare to represent him as dead.

What does it mean to look at the dead face of Christ as we wait for Easter? And why, after Easter, do we still have images of him as dead? James Alison stresses that the Resurrection is not just another stage in the life of Jesus and that he has put death behind him. He is now the crucified and risen one. 'The raising of Jesus was the gratuitous giving back of the whole life and death that had ended on Good Friday – the whole of Jesus' humanity includes his human death.'[6] In the Third Easter Preface Jesus is '*agnus qui vivit semper occisus*', 'who lives forever slain'.

This means that he is still among us as expelled and crucified. He said to Paul on the road to Damascus, 'Why do you persecute me?' Christ's body is still cast out among the poor, and all those who live in desolation. He is among us as powerless as well as triumphant. So the Seven Last Words are not just of Jesus' past, belonging to a previous moment of his life that is over. It is not only we who may sometimes cry out, 'My God, my God, why have you forsaken me?' Christ still utters that cry in us. This dead face challenges all those whose images speak of power and domination, beginning with Caesar, whose face was on the coins that Jesus examined, to tyrants such as Saddam Hussein, whose images used to be seen everywhere in Iraq. David Ford wrote, 'It is clear that the face of this victim of the political and religious powers, remembered as crucified, was bound to be a continuing challenge to all other icons of power and authority.'[7]

In the Old Testament the supreme blessing is for God's face to smile on us. 'Let thy face shine on thy servant; save me in thy steadfast love' (Psalm 31.16). In the Israel Museum in Jerusalem, there is a tiny bit of leather which is 2,500 years old.[8] It contains the oldest biblical text in existence, written in a Hebrew script that was already obsolete by the time of Jesus. It is the words that Aaron used to bless the people of Israel: 'May the Lord bless you and keep you. May the Lord make his face shine upon you and be gracious to you. May the Lord turn his face towards you and give you peace' (Numbers 6.24–26). It took five hundred years for the words on this bit of dried leather to become flesh and blood in the face of Jesus. Before Christ we could not see God and live. We begged that God would smile at us, but we could not look back. Now at the end of his life, we gaze on his dead face. Now it is God who cannot reciprocate the gaze. This is the supreme vulnerability of God in Christ. All friendship is between equals. Our friendship with God means that the previous inequality of gazes must be overthrown. We are not just seen; we see as well.

David Ford also sees in this dead face a call for us to responsibility.

> It represents the full person of Jesus Christ, but in an absence which demands a comparable responsibility. It signifies simultaneously the ultimate carrying out of a responsibility and the complete handing over of it. Before this dead face one can recognize both someone who gave himself utterly for God and for us: it is being dead for us, being absent for us, being one who creates by his death a limitless sphere of responsibility for us. As in Jesus' parables of the master who goes away and leaves stewards in charge, the dead face is the embodiment of a call to responsibility in absence.[9]

He compares this to St Thérèse of Liseux's picture of Jesus asleep in the boat; the disciples must take responsibility and not wake him up.

I am not sure that I would speak so much of Jesus' absence as of his presence through us. The dead face summons us to responsibility because, as St Teresa of Avila said, he has now no feet but ours, no hands but ours and no mouth but ours. On Easter Sunday the Word rose from the dead. After the Ascension, when Jesus is no longer among us as a human being among others, then we are the ones who go on breaking the silence of humanity's tombs.

Audre Lorde, a black American writer, was diagnosed with breast cancer, and facing death confronted her with all the times that she had been silent.

> In becoming forcibly and essentially aware of my mortality, and of what I wished and wanted for my life, however short it might be, priorities and omissions became strongly etched in a merciless light, and what I most regretted were my silences. Of what had I ever been afraid? To question or to speak as I believed could have meant pain, or death. But we all hurt in so many different ways, all the time, and pain will either change or end. Death, on the other hand, is the final silence. And that might be coming quickly, now, without regard for whether I had ever spoken what needed to be said, or had only betrayed myself into small silences, while I planned someday to speak, or waited for someone else's words.[10]

Yves Congar, OP, said, in a wonderful phrase, 'La Bible est virilisante,' 'The Bible is virilizing.' In the face of death, it offers a strong, brave word. The Bible is filled with crazy, full-blooded, passionate men and women, who speak strong words, from Abraham to St Paul. Would we let them into our seminaries and novitiates? Might we not consider them rather unsafe? Would they get past our psychological tests? One never knows what they might sound off about.

Every time we refrain from speaking a strong, courageous word, then we are colluding with the silence of the tomb, the forces of death. Some speaking requires heroism, since it may lead directly to our own death. When Pierre Claverie, the Dominican Bishop of Oran, realized that he was likely to be assassinated by Islamic terrorists, his priests and friends tried to persuade him to keep silent. One of them said to him just before his death, 'I believe that you talk too much. We have need of you.' Pierre replied, 'I cannot be silent. I can be a witness to the truth.' [11] He knew that speaking meant death. That is not the case for us in Britain. There are other pressures that may require almost as much courage to face, even within the Church.

Often we are silenced by the fear that we will not be understood. If we dare to open up 'a can of worms', then we will be misrepresented. The press will get us wrong and our mailbag will be full of angry letters. Maybe we feel that we have not yet found the right words. It is safer to say nothing for the moment, or to hope that someone else will speak. We have to dare to try to find a word, even if it is not quite the right word. We need not be afraid to get it wrong the first time around, because if the Holy Spirit is poured upon the Church, then the Church will not be easily led astray. We must dare to have the humility to say a partial, fumbling word that may help the People of God to arrive at the truth. We need the courage to speak and the humility to know that we may be wrong.

We may be inhibited by respect for authority within the Church, or feel that others should be inhibited by a respect for our own authority. Then we must remember St Catherine of Siena who dared to tell the truth even to popes. She dared tell popes what God wanted them to do. She wrote to Urban VI: 'My dearest *babbo*, forgive my presumption in saying what I've said – what I am compelled by gentle first Truth to say. This is his will, father; this is what he is asking of you!' [12] And when another Pope seemed unhappy with this freedom, she wrote to him that she and her followers would speak the truth 'wherever it pleases God, even to your holiness.' [13] This is not the easy presumption of those who love confrontation and delight to be reprimanded by the Vatican. They are words of someone who deeply respected authority, and who hated to be drawn into conflict. In the Church today there is far too much silence. Czeslaw Milosz, in his acceptance speech for the Nobel Prize for Literature in 1980, said, 'In a room where people unanimously maintain a conspiracy of silence, one word of truth sounds like a pistol shot.'

The courage to speak is ultimately founded upon the courage to listen. Do we dare to listen to the young with their doubts and questions? Do we dare to listen to people who have other theological opinions than ours? Do we dare to listen to people who feel alienated from the Church? Do we listen to those whose lives may appear to place them on the edge, because they are divorced and remarried or gay or living with partners? We will not have the courage to do so unless we have listened in silence to the most disturbing voice of all, that of our God. If we can be silent before God and hear his Word which rose from the dead, then no silence will imprison us in any tomb.

1   *Liquid Modernity*, Cambridge, 2000, p. 76.
2   *Waiting for God*, London, 1951, p. 169.
3   *The Life of Pi*, Edinburgh, 2002, p. 208.
4   *The Writing Life*, New York, 1989, p. 75.
5   *Real Presences: Is there Anything in What we Say?*, London, 1989, p. 232.
6   *Knowing Jesus*, London, 1993, p. 20.
7   David F. Ford, *Self and Salvation: Being Transformed*, Cambridge, 1999, p. 208.
8   Jonathan Sacks, *Celebrating Life: Finding Happiness in Unexpected Places*, London, 2000, p. 148.
9   Ford, *Self and Salvation*, p. 206.
10 *Sister Outsider*, California, 1984, p. 41, cited by C. Hilkert, *Speaking with Authority*, New York, 2001, p. 135.
11 Jean-Jacques Pérennès, *Pierre Claverie: Un Algérien par alliance*, Paris, 2000, p. 358.
12 Letter to Gregory XI, (T255) 18–22 June 1376, trans. Suzanne Noffke, Vol II, *The Letters of St Catherine of Siena*, Tempe, 2001; cited by Hilkert, *Speaking with Authority*, p. 56.
13 Ibid. T305, p. 72.

Our Word

Beyond Violence[1]

On the cross we look upon Christ who is crucified and risen. The dead face of Christ summons us to responsibility. We are the ones who must speak and break the silence. Because he is risen then we may have confidence, because he is with us until the end of time. At the Last Supper Jesus did not just give us his body. He also handed over to us the telling of the story of his life, death and resurrection. The Gospels, including the Seven Last Words, are the early community's acceptance of that responsibility. How are we to exercise it today?

I have suggested that the Seven Last Words of Jesus do not just offer us a particular interpretation of the meaning of human life. What is at issue is whether human existence has any ultimate meaning at all. These last words of Jesus ultimately underpin our faith in the value of words, all attempts to understand who we are and where we are going. 'All things were made through him, and without him was not anything made that was made. In him was life, and the life was the light of human beings' (John 1.3f.). And so all those who struggle to understand the meaning of our lives, and who cherish words and their meaning, may be our friends and allies. We shall disagree with them sometimes but, with the grace of God, in ways that will help us to understand more deeply the Word of God. Yet often we have told the story of Christ's passion, death and resurrection in ways that have inflicted violence on people of other faiths, especially the Jews.

Since the Enlightenment and until recently, it has looked as if religion was losing influence and disappearing from its central place in society. Secularization appeared to make differences of belief relatively unimportant, traces of earlier superstition about to be swallowed up by modernity. September 11 has confronted us violently with the return of religion to the centre of the stage. Nearly everywhere where there is violence we can see the clash of religions. Can we Christians find ways of telling the story of Christ on the cross that may bring peace and diminish violence? Can we retell these Seven Last Words in ways that will heal our relations with Judaism and Islam?

All the Abrahamic faiths are marked by violence. As Jonathan Sacks, the Chief Rabbi, points out, 'the first recorded act of religious worship leads directly to the first murder',[2] that of Abel by Cain. The Exodus of Israel leaves the firstborn of Egypt dead in their beds and their warriors drowned on the seashore. The Christian story climaxes in a brutal execution. Our faiths cannot be sanitized. We can never tell a story of Jesus dying in bed as a contented old man. But how can we as Christians tell of his passion and death in a way that does no violence to others? The paradox is that Judaism has deepened its faith by facing the apparent powerlessness of the God who brought them out of Egypt with a strong arm. For Christianity it has been the contrary. We have had to struggle with how the followers of the powerless Christ can have wreaked such violence on other people. For Judaism the question has been how to tell its story in the light of violence endured; for us, it has been in the light of violence inflicted. This is why the Holocaust is such a crisis for both our faiths.

I wish to look, briefly and superficially, at three violent moments: the conquest of the Americas, the Holocaust and September 11. I will ask how each moment provokes a retelling of the death and resurrection of Christ. Each of these traumas has invited us to purify our story of its potential for violence. Each invites us to change our understanding of the actors in the drama. Maybe we have discovered that we were playing other roles than we had thought. It is as if, reading *King Lear*, we had thought that we were Cordelia only to discover that we are Goneril and Regan. Each of these events changes the way in which we understand how our time relates to the time of that story, how we live within its temporal structure. I would also just like to hint at how both Judaism and Islam may help us to retell this story more beautifully and truly. Judaism has been, as it were, the 'other' within western Christian civilization; Islam has been the external 'other' for so long, and until recently. Maybe both can help us to tell our Christian story aright.

The Conquest of the Americas

The conquest of the Americas questioned a way of telling the story of the death and resurrection of Christ which is summed up in the phrase: *Extra Ecclesiam nulla salus*, 'Outside the Church no salvation'. The medieval Church believed that the resurrection of Christ marked a new time for all of humanity. After this time no one had any excuse for not believing in Christ. The whole world had encountered the gospel. If Jews and Muslims rejected Christ, then they sinned. When one read the passion narratives, one read the story of one's contemporaries. The Jewish neighbours were the people who rejected Christ and called for his blood. The gospel narrative told of 'us' and 'them', and drew clear lines between those inside and those outside. On the street one could see those who had stood at the foot of the cross and mocked our Lord.

The conquest of the Americas began to jolt the Church out of this story. There was the raw shock of the encounter with millions of people who had never heard of Christ, and had no part in that story. How could they have rejected Christ? It was the shock of reality. Albert Pigge, a Flemish theologian who was two years old when Columbus arrived in the Americas, wrote,

> If you say that by now the gospel of Christ has been sufficiently prom-
> ulgated in the whole world, so that ignorance can no longer excuse anyone
> – reality itself refutes you, because every day now numberless nations
> are being discovered among whom, or among their forefathers, no trace
> is found of the gospel ever having been preached, so that to all those
> people up to our time Christ was simply unheard of.[3]

It was above all the Dominicans at the University of Salamanca in Spain who challenged the old story, and surely this was because they were in close contact with their brethren in Hispaniola, what is now the Dominican Republic and Haiti. Their brethren shared with them the violence of the encounter with the indige-nous people. The shock of reality was not merely the existence of these people but the violence that they endured at the hands of the Spaniards. One can feel the anger in the words of the famous sermon by Antonio de Montesinos, OP, on the first Sunday of Advent, 1511 when he confronted the Spaniards with their treatment of the Indians: 'Are they not human? Do they not have rational souls? With what right do you make war on them? Are you not obliged to love them as yourselves?' When the colonialists complained to the Prior of S. Domingo, Pedro di Cordoba, he replied that when Antonio preached, the whole community preached. And Bartolome de Las Casas kept alive the fire of indignation through his sizzling reports to his brethren of Spanish cruelty. The Christian Spaniards were idolaters, worshipping gold, and the pagan Indians were Christ crucified.

How did this experience of brutal violence change the way in which the Christian story was told? Back in Salamanca, Francisco de Vitoria questioned whether it is enough just to announce the gospel for people to be culpable of rejecting it. How could they be blamed for rejecting Christ when they see the cruelty of the Christians? He wrote,

It is not sufficiently clear to me that the Christian faith has yet been so put before the indigenous people and announced to them that they are bound to believe it or commit fresh sin. ... I hear of many scandals and cruel crimes and acts of impiety, hence it does not appear that the Christian religion has been preached to them with such sufficient propriety and piety that they are bound to acquiesce in it.[4]

Pigge applied this same principle to the Muslims. If they have never had the gospel convincingly preached, how can they be blamed for rejecting it? These people, the Muslims and the Indians, are being treated no longer just as actors in our narrative of Christ's death and resurrection, with walk-on parts in our story. They are conceived of as subjects, centres of autonomous awareness, looking at us and listening to us and making their own judgements. Furthermore, they are not necessarily playing the parts we had assigned them. For they are Christ crucified and it is the Christians who nail them to the cross.

A second evolution was in the relationship between the narrative and time. St Thomas Aquinas had accepted that Gentiles who lived before the coming of Christ could have been saved by an implicit faith in Christ, but after Christ an explicit faith was necessary. The medieval narrative had a single chronological structure, the time in our Christian history when Christ rose again. Domingo Soto, another Salamancan Dominican, argued that the American Indians lived within their own time and for them the moment of decision was not the date that Christ rose from the dead but the moment that they encountered him. Before that they could be saved by implicit faith. It is the time of their narrative and not of a single universal chronology that matters. Again the individual becomes a centre of his or her own narrative rather than just an actor in a single universal tale.

These may seem to be two small theological nuances, a slight opening of the doors of paradise to those who are not Christians. But one may also read them as a loosening of the Church's hold on its foundational narrative. The story of Christ's death and resurrection becomes less an absolute possession of the Church and more a story that we offer to those who live it in their own way and in ways that we may not have anticipated. The awareness of the violence of this moment produced a slight opening of our universal story to difference, to respect for the stranger.

The Holocaust

The unutterable violence of the Holocaust shook our confidence in the possibility of telling any story of faith at all. How could the Jews tell a story of the God who does marvellous deeds, when he did nothing at this moment? How could Christians tell the story of our powerless Saviour on a cross when some of his followers had complicity in this violence? What story could either faith tell anymore? Reflecting on Auschwitz, E. L. Doctorow wrote,

> To presume to contain God in this unknowing story of ours, to hold Him, circumscribe Him, the author of everything we can conceive and everything we cannot conceive ... in *our* story of *Him*? Of her? Of whom? What in the name of our faith – what in God's name – do we think we are talking about? [5]

Rabbi Irving Greenberg said, 'No statement, theological or otherwise, should be made that would not be credible in the presence of burning children.'[6] What can any of us say in the presence of burning babies? Once again we see a crisis which threatens our trust in all words.

When we listen to the recitations of the passion narratives during Holy Week, there are phrases that have become almost impossible for us to bear, especially from the Gospels of Matthew and John. How can we repeat these words: 'And all the people answered, "His blood be on us and on our children!"' (Matthew 27.25)? When we hear such passages we may be tempted simply to dismiss them as subsequent corruptions of an initially pure and authentic Christianity: the original story has been deformed by later prejudice and unchristian hatred. Such delving behind the texts for some earlier story that is innocent and pure is as futile and fruitless as the attempt to base one's faith on the historical Jesus. One always ends up with what one wants to find. Rather, we must accept that it is precisely the horror of the Holocaust that may help us, tentatively and humbly, to understand the story of Christ better now. Rowan Williams, speaking of the individual search for identity, wrote that 'the self is not a substance one unearths by peeling away layers until one gets to the core, but an integrity one struggles to bring into existence'.[7] Similarly, the story that gives the Church its own sense of identity is not one to be attained by peeling away the layers until one gets to the original core. After the Holocaust we are involved in the struggle to bring it to Word newly.

The Jews can no longer be seen just as actors in our story, playing the roles that our story gives them. We have mythologized the Jews and given them walk-on parts in a story they do not recognize as their own. As one scholar said, we have used the Jews to think with.[8] This narratival violence was complicit with the monstrous violence of the Holocaust. But our Jewish elder brothers and sisters have their own story to tell, of election and survival, as witnesses of God's fidelity. The violence that we have inflicted shows that we have not told well our own story, of the man who turned the other cheek. What happened at the Holocaust revealed the potential for violence in the way that we understood what happened to him.

This means that the Jews even until today are an intrinsic part of our identity. We cannot say who we are apart from the recognition of who they are. When John Paul II addressed the Jewish community in the synagogue of Rome in 1986, he said, 'The Jewish religion is not "extrinsic" to us, but in a certain manner, it is "intrinsic" to our religion.'[9] So it belongs to the proper telling of our Christian story that it is not the only story to tell. This was explicitly recognized in 2002 by the Pontifical Biblical Commission:

> Christians can and ought to admit that the Jewish reading of the Bible is a possible one, and in continuity with the Jewish Sacred Scriptures from the Second Temple period, a reading analogous to the Christian reading which developed in parallel fashion. Both readings are bound up with the vision of their respective faiths, of which the readings are the result and expression. Consequently, both are irreducible.[10]

This represents a vast sea change in our understanding of our universal story. Paradoxically, it can only be heard as properly universal if it gives a place to their particular story. We must hear the good news of Judaism if our gospel is to be good news too. Our own DNA is a double helix, of Judaism and Christianity.[11]

Finally we recognize Christ's story as Jewish. The Jews do not only have the role of being the accusers. They may occupy all the roles. They are the disciples, and they are Jesus, as well as the crowd and the high priests. The accusations, the words that we dread to hear, were words of a debate within Judaism. The violence of these words is that of a family argument, like the violent words of the prophets against Israel. In so far as we allocate any special role to the Jews, then after the Holocaust it must above all be that of the victim, the crucified one. They are not 'the God killers' but God's chosen one, the one cast out.

11 September 2001

Today we also live in the shadow of a more recent violent moment, 11 September 2001. Jonathan Sacks described that as the moment 'when two universalist cultures, global capitalism and an extremist form of Islam, each profoundly threatening to the other, met and clashed.'[12] The violence of that terrible day confronted us with the hidden violence of our economic system which, as it is presently structured, does indeed bring wealth to millions but also produces poverty and an ever increasing inequality. Two thirds of the inhabitants of our global village live in the slums, on less than the subsidy which is given to every cow in the European Union.

On 9/11 that violence came home to us. As Rowan Williams wrote,

> Every transaction in the developed economies of the West can be interpreted as an act of aggression against the economic losers in the worldwide game. However much we protest that this is a caricature, this is how it is experienced. And we have to begin to understand how such a perception is part of the price that we pay for the benefits of globalization.[13]

This violence is the fruit of modern global capitalism. It would make no sense to be against the market as such, but its present operation is linked to the interests of the powerful nations. And historically its development had deep links with a certain form of Christian universalism. It can all be neatly symbolized by the opening of the Suez Canal. The company founded in 1858 to build it was called *La Compagnie Universelle*. The papal nuncio gave a rousing speech in which he appears to compare the opening of the Canal to the creation of the world, as the breath of God hovers over the waters. All of humanity is being gathered into unity. '*O Occident! O Orient! Rapprochez, regardez, reconnaissez, saluez, étreignez-vous!*' Needless to say, all this is happening under the guidance of the Christian God: 'The cross is erect respected by everyone in the face of the crescent.'[14] The cross here represents a universality which is deeply linked with the imperialism of the Christian West.

So the violence of 9/11 must make us pause and wonder whether we must not go further in rethinking how we tell the story of Christ's death and resurrection. Last April I visited the Al Hazar mosque with the Prior of our community in Cairo. After prayers we sat and talked with three young men who were studying at the University. One of them, Amir, has remained in contact with me, especially during the Iraqi war. It has been beautiful to see this devout young Muslim sharing his longing for peace. I felt welcomed into this stranger's heart and life.

When I read Louis Massignon, perhaps the greatest Western expert on Islam in the last century, I understood a little of the special quality of that relationship. He explains how Islamic hospitality brought him back home to his Christian faith. The welcome that he received in this same university and in Mesopotamia opened him to welcome the divine stranger into his life. He developed through his studies of Islam a theory of 'sacred hospitality' in which one even offers to share the stranger's sufferings. Charles de Foucauld talked of exactly the same experience of hospitality. Pierre Claverie spoke of being a guest in the house of Islam. This led Muslims to offer him a protective wall of security when his life was threatened by extremists. This deep sense of hospitality for the stranger is in violent contrast with our world of the global market. The global market offers no hospitality. It is ruthless. And all over the world Muslims from traditional cultures feel violated by the merciless culture of the market. Markets, yes; the Arab world was built up by trading. But the world as one big market, no.

What are the roots of this Islamic welcome to the stranger, so at odds with the usual image of intolerance? David Burrell of Notre Dame said in a lecture in Cambridge in 2002 that 'the very presence of a stranger elicits a welcoming response from them'. Why?

It may have something to do with the call of the Qur'an, the way it calls for a response from the listener. And since that response takes place in a communal setting, we are then linked together as responders to the creating Word of God, and so begin actively to participate in what is generated in the synergy between call and response.[15]

Although we do not share the same faith, and indeed Muslims regard our revelation as superseded by that of Mohammed, yet we are respected by some Muslims as fellow hearers. Perhaps the profound Islamic sense of the transcendence of God may relativize any exclusive religious identity.

A fascinating article by Dr Tim Winter of Cambridge University grounds this openness in the absence in Islam of a covenant with a particular community of people, a people set apart. He refers to a Qur'anic passage (7.172) which 'does speak of a primordial covenant between God and every human soul, sealed before the creation of the world. In Muslim reflection, Islam is not a compact with a particular section of humanity, but is the eschatological restoration of this primordial pledge, one of whose "signs" is the Hajj to the House which is "for all mankind" (2:125).'[16] So in that sense Islam may not be exclusive. Its universalism is not the universal claim for a particular people. There are no anonymous Muslims, merely human beings who are called to acknowledge the unicity and justice of God as revealed by Mohammed. God has sent prophets to all nations to make known his will. At the last judgement some Muslims believe that Moses will plead for Jews, Jesus for Christians and Mohammed for everyone. Islam supersedes Judaism and Christianity not by embodying a new people of God, but by claiming to be the uncorrupt disclosure of the truth of God's will for all human beings.

The Christian West has been from almost the beginning that 'other' over and against which Islam has defined itself. So it is not surprising that it was an extremist form of Islam that made a violent protest against the economic system that is centred in the West. Would it be entirely crazy to dream that Islam might help us to understand all those others who suffer deprivation and misery at our hands? Islam might even help us to take another step further into the mystery of the Christian story by which we live. It might help us to tell our story in a way that respects the stranger as a fellow listener to the Word. It might teach us hospitality towards the strangers of our global village. It might lead us to become more humble when we talk about ourselves as 'the People of God'. It might loosen our presumptive grip on the story of Christ. We must share it as Christ shared himself. If we are to make disciples of all nations, then we must become disciples, students, ourselves.

As a Christian I do found my faith on the death and resurrection of Christ as the definitive moment in God's relationship with humanity. We saw that the Holocaust has transformed our understanding of that event. We discovered that the DNA which is our foundational narrative is a double helix, which links us from the inside with Judaism. The crisis of September 11 may lead us further. Islam has a different relationship with us. I am not suggesting a triple helix! Yet it too may teach us how to tell our own story better.

Think of the cross by which we sign ourselves. Above I pointed out that the first known representation of the cross is on the doors of S. Sabina where I lived in Rome for nine years. It dates from 432. Is it a coincidence that we only dared to represent this symbol of imperial cruelty when the Roman Empire had just become Christian? This cross became the symbol of the aggression of the crusaders. We are living a slow education in the meaning of the cross and of the one who 'humbled himself and became obedient unto death, even death on a cross' (Philippians 2.8). In Hispaniola, Las Casas saw the indigenous people crucified by Spaniards. In the Holocaust we have seen our Jewish brothers and sisters crucified on this same cross. Maybe now, after 9/11, we may be more aware of how we are at the centre of an economic system which is crucifying much of humanity, and Islam may help us to see how better to tell our story as one which reaches to all our fellow human beings.

Rowan Williams wrote after September 11,

Can we think about our focal symbol, the cross of Jesus, and try to rescue it from its frequent fate as the banner of our wounded righteousness? If Jesus is indeed what God communicates to us, God's language for us, his cross is always both ours and not ours; not a magnified sign of our own suffering, but the mark of God's work in and through the deepest vulnerability; not a martyr's triumphant achievement, but something that is there for all human sufferers because it belongs to no human cause.[17]

We have listened together to the Seven Last Words of Christ on the cross. They promise us forgiveness for the violence that we have committed, Paradise when all seems lost, communion when it has been broken. They embrace us in our deepest desolation, show us our God begging for a gift from us; they invite us to open ourselves to the perfection of love, and promise us final rest. Perhaps September 11 invites us to hear those words with the ears of all those whom we exclude and crush, whether they share our faith or another or none at all. For Christ on the cross is not someone whom we own, but all of humanity crucified.

A month before his assassination, the Dominican Bishop of Oran, Pierre Claverie said: 'The Church fulfils her vocation when she is present on the fractures that crucify humanity in its flesh and unity. Jesus died spread out between heaven and earth, his arms stretched out to gather in the children of God scattered by the sin which separates them, isolates them, and sets them up against each other and against God himself. He placed himself on the lines of

fracture born of this sin. In Algeria we are on one of these seismic lines that cross
the world: Islam/the West, North/South, rich/poor. And we are truly in our place
here, because it is in this place that one can glimpse the light of the Resurrection.'[18]

1 Much of this section is taken from my article, '"Go and make disciples of all
   nations." Proclaiming the Kingdom or Religious Imperialism', *New
   Blackfriars*, July/August 2003, pp. 323–34.
2 *The Dignity of Difference: How to Avoid the Clash of Civilizations*, London
   and New York, 2002, p. 46.
3 Francis A. Sullivan, SJ, *Salvation Outside the Church? Tracing the History of
   the Catholic Response*, New York, 1992, p. 80.
4 Ibid., p. 72.
5 From 'Heist' quoted by Robert W. Bullock, 'After Auschwitz: Jews, Judaism
   and Christian Worship' in *'Good News' after Auschwitz: Christian Faith
   within a Post-Holocaust World*, eds. Carol Rittner and John K. Roth, Macon,
   2001, p. 69.
6 'Cloud of Smoke, Pillar of Fire: Judaism, Christianity, and Modernity after the
   Holocaust' in *Auschwitz: Beginning of a New Era?*, ed. Eva Fleischner, New
   York, 1977, p. 23.
7 *On Christian Theology*, Oxford, 2000, p. 240.
8 Quoted by Rowan Williams, *Writing in the Dust: Reflections on 11th
   September and its Aftermath*, London, 2002, p. 65. He does not mention who
   this scholar is.
9 Quoted in *The Jewish People and their Sacred Scriptures in the Christian
   Bible*, Pontifical Biblical Commission, Rome, 2002, p. 196.
10 Ibid., p. 51.
11 I owe this image to comments by Dr Janet Martin Soskice.
12 *The Dignity of Difference*, p. 20.
13 *Writing in the Dust*, p. 58 (n.17).
14 Edward Said, *Orientalism: Western Conceptions of the Orient*, London, 1995, p. 91.
15 I am grateful to David Burrell for sending me a copy of this lecture.
16 'The last Trump Card' in *Studies in Interreligious Dialogue*, 9/1999/2, pp. 133–
   155.
17 *Writing in the Dust*, p. 77f.
18 Pérennès, *Pierre Claverie*, p. 301.